W9-CEL-765

Rosa M. Curto

Draw the Magic Fairy

Draw the Magic Red Fairy

Enslow Elementary

an imprint of

Enslow Publishers, Inc.

40 Industrial Road
Box 398
Berkeley Heights, NJ 07922
USA

http://www.enslow.com

Tasty Cookies

2

The red fairy is baking cookies.

They come in many different flavors and shapes.

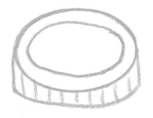

Mmmmmmm! They smell delicious!

3

Fresh Bread

Look at all
these loaves
of bread!

4

The red fairy also enjoys baking bread.
She makes long, round, filled, and seeded loaves
of bread. There are so many different kinds!

5

The red fairy always amazes her
friends with a new kind of bread.

Cushions

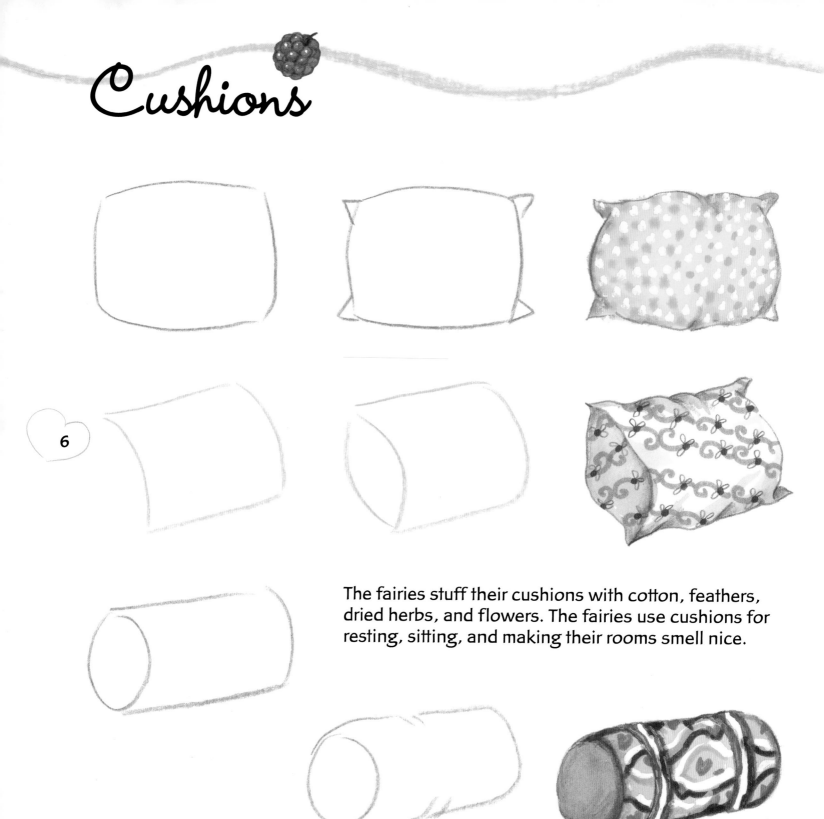

6

The fairies stuff their cushions with *cotton*, feathers, dried herbs, and flowers. The fairies use cushions for resting, sitting, and making their rooms smell nice.

These cushions are decorated
and sewn with silk thread.

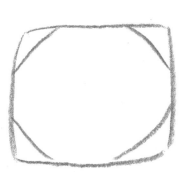 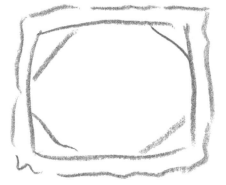 

Garden Tools

Fairies love working in the garden.
They use:

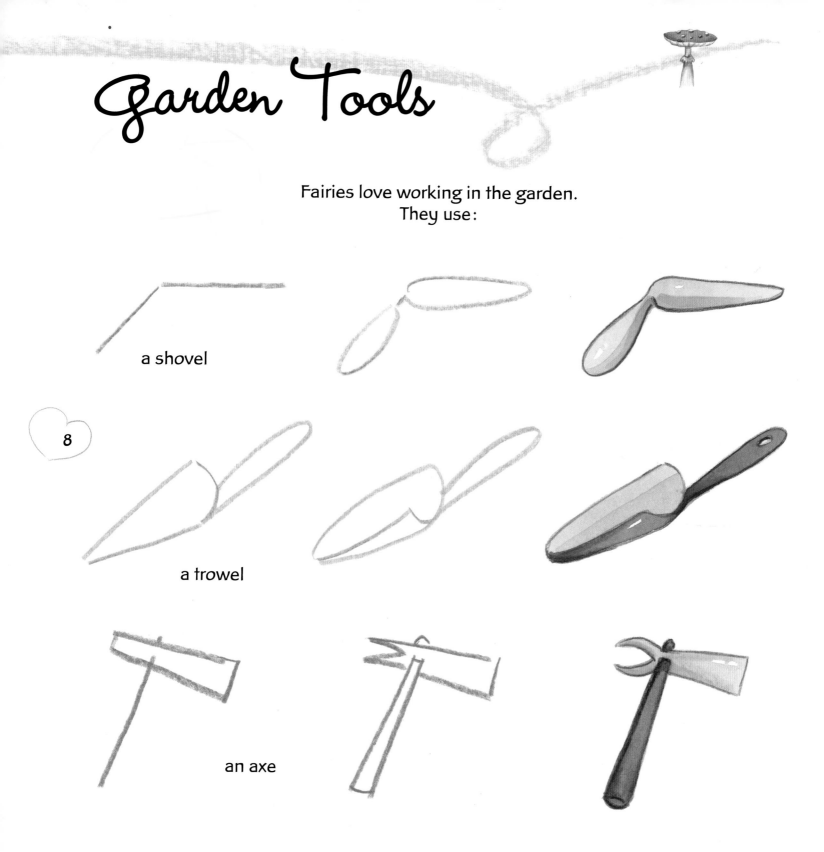

a shovel

a trowel

an axe

a watering can

a hoe

The red fairy is so happy to see the first flowers bloom!

and a wheelbarrow.

Reusing and Recycling

an empty nest

10

a nutshell

a glass bead

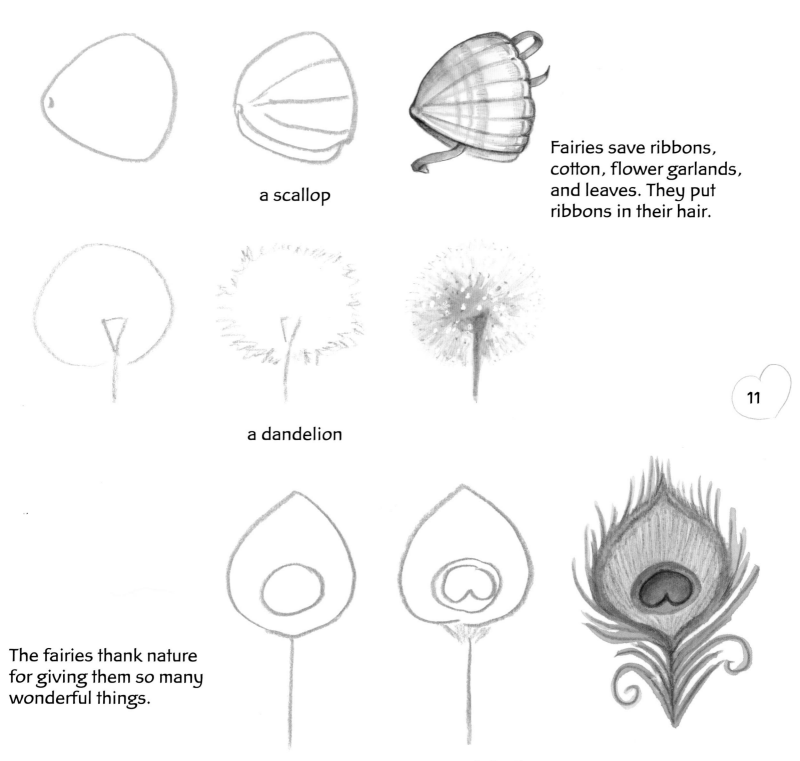

a scallop

Fairies save ribbons, cotton, flower garlands, and leaves. They put ribbons in their hair.

a dandelion

11

The fairies thank nature for giving them so many wonderful things.

a peacock feather

Dresses and Parasols

The fairies' dresses are very comfortable.

Fairies do not like wearing heavy clothing with too many decorations. The red fairy and her friends always dress in light, pretty dresses.

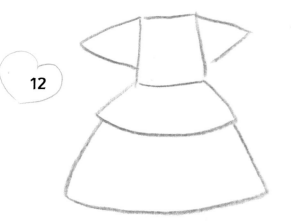

They make parasols from
bell-shaped flowers. They use
parasols to shade themselves
from the sun. They also use
bell-shaped flowers as umbrellas
when it rains or snows.

13

Fruits of the Forest

Blueberries, raspberries, cherries . . .

14

Have you ever tasted a cherry tart?
Or raspberry ice cream?

. . . cranberries, blackberries, and strawberries

15

Mushrooms

stem

gills

cap

The forest is full of mushrooms. Mushrooms have a very special smell.
Fairies can smell them from very far away.

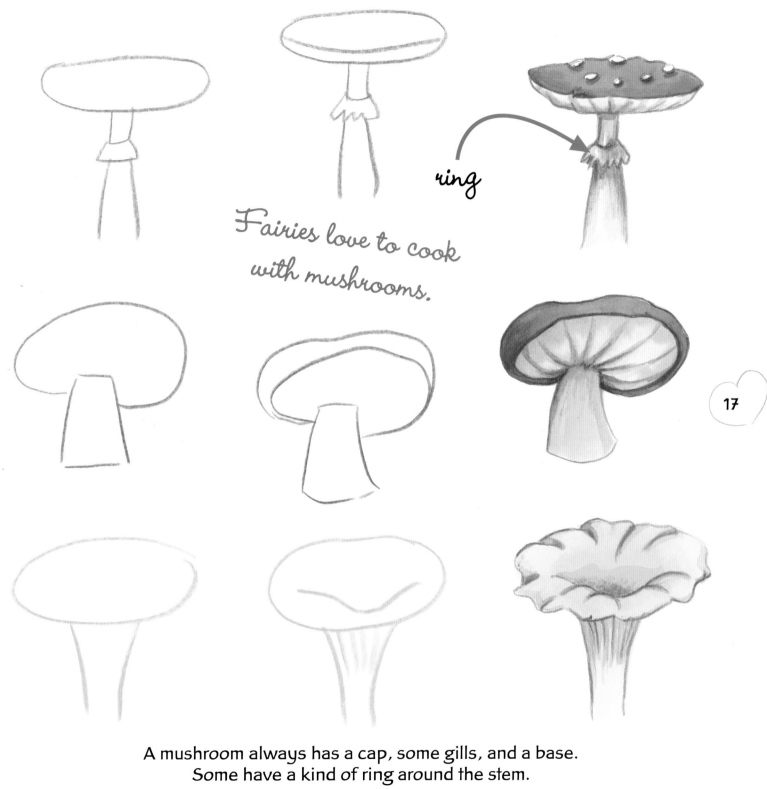

Fairies love to cook with mushrooms.

ring

17

A mushroom always has a cap, some gills, and a base.
Some have a kind of ring around the stem.

Different Kinds of Beetles

Here are eight beetles. They belong to the insect family.

18

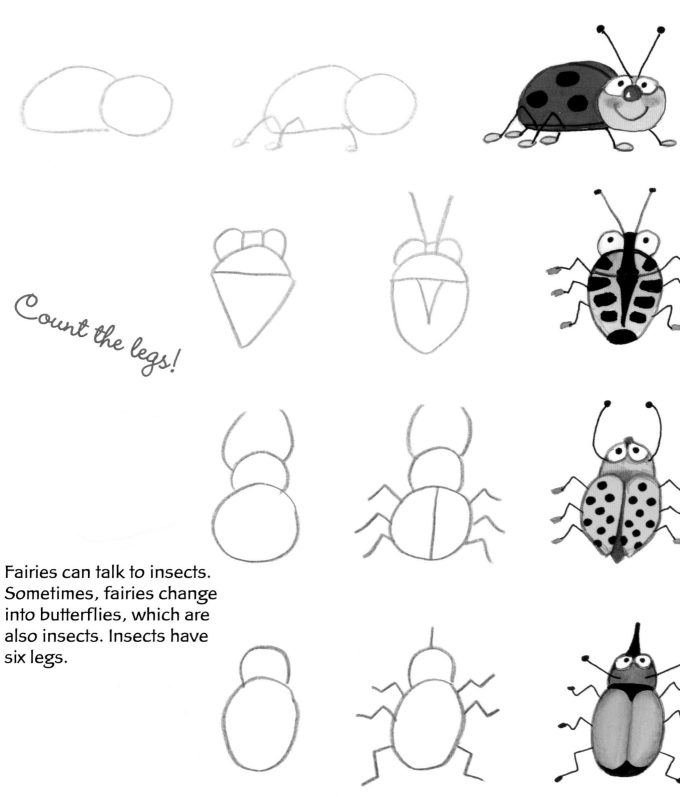

Count the legs!

Fairies can talk to insects.
Sometimes, fairies change
into butterflies, which are
also insects. Insects have
six legs.

19

Colorful Fish

In three steps, you can draw a fish.

Here are six examples.

They are all very *good* friends of
Fairy Melissa, who loves to swim.

Eddie the Eagle

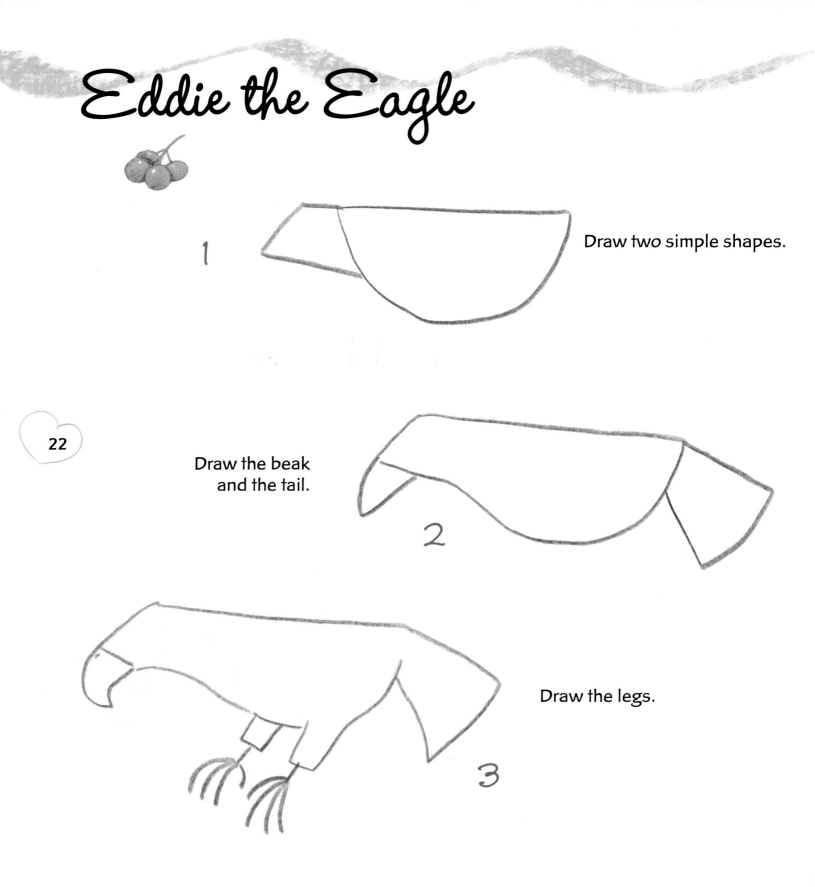

1 Draw two simple shapes.

Draw the beak
and the tail.

2

Draw the legs.

3

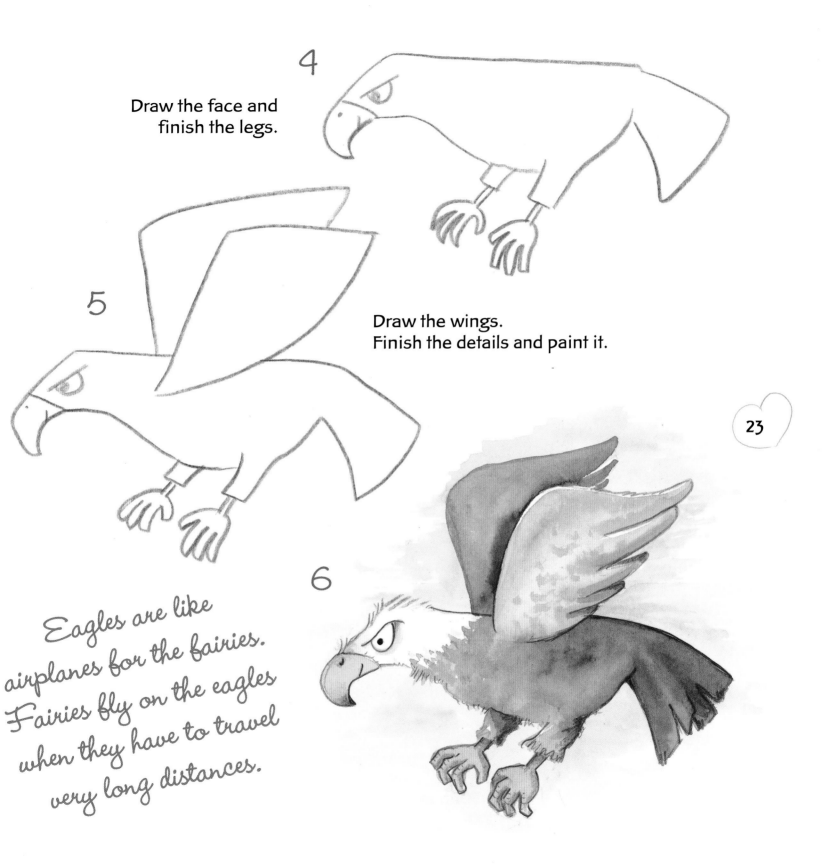

4

Draw the face and
finish the legs.

5

Draw the wings.
Finish the details and paint it.

6

Eagles are like
airplanes for the fairies.
Fairies fly on the eagles
when they have to travel
very long distances.

The Fairy of Small Spells

1 Draw four simple shapes.

2 Outline the hat and the sleeve.

Draw an arm and the legs.

3

4

Draw the other arm and the wings on her back.

Finish the dress.

Finish the arms and legs.
Draw the shoes.

5

6

7

Finish the details and paint her!

This little fairy always wears a hat and never forgets her magic wand.

The Red Fairy

Draw three simple shapes.

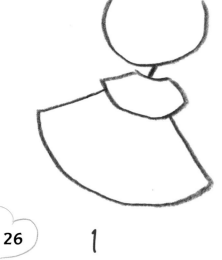

1

Outline the hair.

2

Draw the nose.

3

4

Finish the hairstyle and the dress.

5

Outline where
the arms and legs
will *go*.

Draw the face and finish
the arms and legs.

6

Finish the details
and paint her!

7

The red fairy has short dark hair.

Fairy Valerie

1

Draw a shape for the head
and another for the body.

2

Outline the hair.

3

Outline the sleeve.

4

Draw the arms
and the hands.

5

Draw the legs
and the shoes.

6

Finish the dress
and draw the wings.

7

Draw the face.
Finish the arms and legs.
Paint her.

She is generous and gives the fruit to hungry animals.

Fairy Annabelle

Draw two simple shapes.

1

Outline the neck and the hair.

2

Add details to the hair and draw the sleeves of the dress.

3

Mark the places where the hands, legs, and feet will go.

4

5

Draw the ears and finish the legs.

Draw the wings.

6

Fairy Annabelle knows a lot about the stars and the sky.

7

Finish the details and paint her!

She loves to fly. She is very graceful. Her feet hardly ever touch the ground.

A

B

Look at fairy faces A and B. What is the difference between them? The distance between the eyes can change the face.

Drawing Faces

What are the differences between face 1 and face 2?
And between faces 2 and 3?
And between faces 1 and 3?

1

2

3

Look!
Now only the nose is different!

The hairstyles of these three heads
are different.

Now you try!

Draw a fairy and see what happens
when you make some changes.

Little Lamps and Garlands

Little lamps light up the fairies' night parties.

34

They are the loveliest lights you have ever seen.

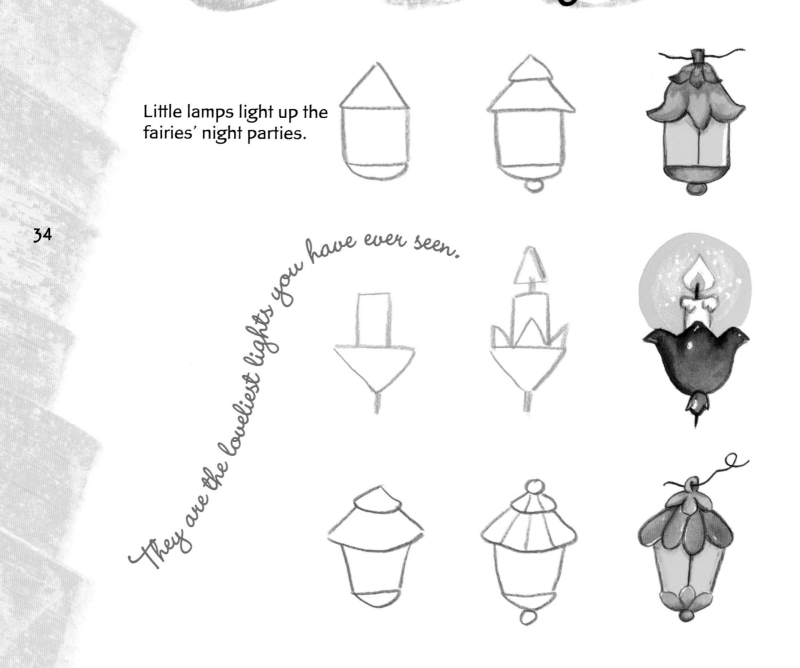

The red fairy makes a garland of dried leaves.

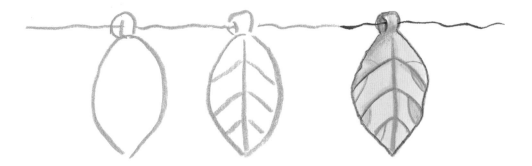

To make garlands, you will need brightly colored pieces of wide ribbon.
Sew a hem at the back of each piece. Thread string through them.

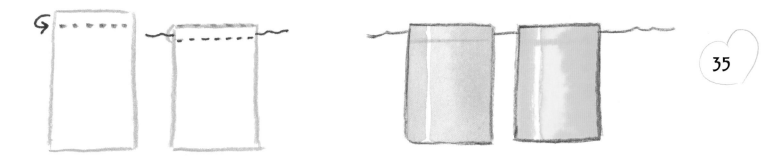

You can also make garlands from colored paper.

You can paint the paper yourself.

Enslow Elementary, an imprint of Enslow Publishers, Inc.
Enslow Elementary® is a registered trademark of Enslow Publishers, Inc.

English edition copyright © 2014 by Enslow Publishers, Inc.

Original title of the book in Catalan: *DIBUIXANT EL MÓN DE LES FADES 3*
Copyright © GEMSER PUBLICATIONS, S.L., 2012
C/ Castell, 38; Teià (08329) Barcelona, Spain (World Rights)
Tel: 93 540 13 53
E-mail: info@mercedesros.com
Web site: http://www.mercedesros.com
Author and illustrator: Rosa Maria Curto

Library of Congress Cataloging-in-Publication Data

Curto, Rosa Maria.
 [Dibuixant el món de les fades. 3. English]
 Draw the magic red fairy / Rosa M. Curto.
     pages cm — (Draw the magic fairy)
 Summary: "Learn how to draw the world of the red fairy, including her other fairy friends, different animals, food, tools, clothes, and much more"—Provided by publisher.
 ISBN 978-0-7660-4267-4
 1. Drawing—Technique—Juvenile literature. 2. Fairies in art—Juvenile literature. I. Title.
 NC655.C87313 2013
 741.2—dc23
                                      2012030437

Future edition:
Paperback ISBN 978-1-4644-0477-1

Printed in China
122012 Leo Paper Group, Heshan City, Guangdong, China
10 9 8 7 6 5 4 3 2 1